HOW TO BECOME
A VOICE OVER ARTIST

HOW TO BECOME A VOICE OVER ARTIST
Copyright © 2014-2017 Natalie Roers
http://www.natalieroers.com/

All rights reserved. No part of this book may be reproduced, stored in a retrieval system or transmitted in any form by any means electronic, mechanical, photocopying, recording or otherwise, except brief extracts for the purpose of review, without the permission of the publisher and copyright owner. The author receives no compensation for the products and services mentioned in this guide.

Cover design by Rob Williams
Edited by Eleonor Gardner

Printed in the United States of America.

HOW TO BECOME A VOICE OVER ARTIST

BY
NATALIE ROERS

TABLE OF CONTENTS

Preface 7
Preparing Yourself Mentally 9
A Few, Quick, Common, Audio Trouble-Shooting
   Tips for Beginners 25
Time to Practice! 29
Classes, Coaches, and Vocal Tips, Oh My!................39
Making a Demo 49
Final Homework..55
Dipping Your Toe in the Auditioning Pool..............59
Booking Your First Job: Congrats, You're Now
   an Accountant!...69
Additional Items to Consider as You Begin
   Booking Jobs 73
Creating an Online Presence 77
Growing a Client Base...81
Starting a Business..87
Spreading Your Wings...89
About the Author 101

PREFACE

Welcome to the world of voice overs! My name is Natalie Roers and I am a full-time voice over artist that makes my living doing voice over work from home. Before I get into how I broke into the voice over business, you may have noticed from my bio that I worked in broadcasting before becoming a work-at-home voice over artist. Don't be intimidated by this detail!

While it may seem like I could have used connections to break into this business, that is indeed, not the case. When I started my voice over career, I was employed by a television station that had me under a non-compete contract, essentially barring me from using my name and reputation to do any commercial work in my area. As such, I built my career using an alias and did absolutely no work in the state where I was known and employed. Not one production company I worked for was aware of my real identity until my voice over career was fully established, and a reasonable amount of time had passed after deciding to leave television.

Yes, I did gain experience talking on camera and using editing equipment during my time as a radio and television personality, but becoming an audio expert and running a studio were completely new to me. I learned these things with just as much frustration as you probably will. Well, maybe not--you at least have this guide.

Best,

Natalie

PREPARING YOURSELF MENTALLY

"You record commercials at home? You mean, people pay you to do that?" These are generally the first two questions people ask me when I tell them that I'm a voice over artist. When I answer, yes, the follow-up usually goes something like this: "Well, that's easy…you just talk into a mic and you get paid? I could do that."

Let's get real. Getting a paying voice over job is much like selling a few cupcakes at a bake sale. No, it's not that hard to do. There is, however, a very big difference between selling a few cupcakes at a bake sale and building a self-sustaining cupcake business. If you want to make a living doing voice overs, yes, it does involve quite a bit more than just talking into a microphone.

This is a no-fluff, step-by-step guide detailing everything I did from what equipment I used, to how I broke into the business, to how I built my client base to become a full-time home-studio voice over recording artist.

Whether you're simply interested in what the field entails, are looking to do voice overs as a hobby, or are ready to take your voice work to the next level, this guide should answer all of your questions quickly and clearly. This is by no means the only way to break into the biz, but it's what worked for me. I encourage you to read as many different books about this business as you can.

Why would I give a step-by-step guide to potential competition out there? Frankly, not many people will see it all the way through. It takes a long time to build a career in anything. You have to have a thick skin, patience, talent, and a love for the craft. You have to love it enough to work at it daily, without much of a return for quite some time.

For those of you who do follow-through, you were going to do it anyway, so I'm happy to pass on the knowledge that I've gained in the hopes that you pay it forward to another budding talent one day. There are more than enough voice jobs, and more than enough varying vocal styles needed to go around, and the field is only growing, so maybe one day I'll "see" *you* around the auditioning pool. Good luck!

BUILDING A RECORDING SPACE

You mean, I don't just plug a mic into my computer? Again, no, you don't just "talk into a mic" for this job. Before you do anything, you need to make sure you have the right equipment in order to record properly and you need to make sure you know how to use that equipment very well.

Production companies love to work with home-studio voice over talent for two big reasons: it saves them time and it saves them money. Production companies that hire us can get studio-quality recordings without paying to rent studio space. They also don't have to worry about time constraints. If they need audio now, they don't have to wait a few days for an available recording window. This means, before you even start dipping your toe in the auditioning pool (which we'll get to later), you need to know how to run a studio.

When I first got started, I went mid-level in my recording equipment and in setting up my space. Feel free to upgrade when you're doing this for a living, but you want to start with what works well and what won't bankrupt you. The following is what I started out using and what I still used well into my transition going full-time in this field.

The Home-Studio Shopping List

I am often asked for an EXACT list of the equipment I used when I got started (I have since updated this a bit to reflect current technology), so here it is! Please note, you can do your own research and decide what works best for you. Although most home recording equipment operates around the same basic principles, I will be using the equipment listed on the following page for my trouble-shooting tips and examples throughout this guide.

The List:

- **A good desk-top or laptop computer**
- **A desk**
- **A good pair of headphones**
- **Audio-Technica Large Diaphragm Cardioid Condenser Microphone with Shock Mount:** I love the sound quality of these mics for the price. And the cardioid pattern means they reduce sounds coming from the sides and rear of the mic. Just make sure it's facing the right direction when you set it up! If your voice seems really quiet, your mic is facing the wrong way!
- **A desk mic stand**
- **Pop Filter:** These filters attach to the front of your mic and are used to soften "pops" of unwanted breath, such as the rush of fast-moving air that comes out of your mouth on the letter "p" when saying the word "pop."
- **Mixcraft Editing Software:** I've used a lot of editing software and this seems to be the easiest one to use; it

has just what voice over artists need. I did some audio work for Mixcraft (http://www.acoustica.com/mixcraft/) when I was just starting out and was allowed to download their software for free. I have not had any contact with these people since, and make nothing by saying this, but the program is honestly terrific. I'll be using this software for reference when I discuss audio troubleshooting and editing techniques. You can choose whatever you want to use. All editing systems basically have the same stuff--it's all about personal preference. Personally, I loathe Pro-Tools. It's not newbie-friendly, but if you plan to shoot and edit video or produce full musical pieces for your clients in addition to your voice work, Pro-Tools would probably serve you well.

- **M-Audio Fast Track Pro USB interface:** I don't want you to spend too much money, but I also don't want you to waste your money. You cannot buy a mic that plugs right into your computer's USB port. You need to buy an interface to run your mic through first, and then, plug that interface into your computer. There's no way around how bad a USB mic sounds when it comes to promoting yourself as a home studio. You can audition with these mics, sure, but you cannot say you have a professional space if that's what you use. I'll explain this further at the end of this chapter.

- **iTunes:** You will need to have iTunes downloaded on your computer with an icon easily available on your desktop. Not only can you save all your client files in iTunes, you can also bump your files down to different formats like AIFF, WAV, and MP3 if your editing software does not offer all the formats you need.
- **Gmail email account:** Gmail is capable of sending multiple, large audio files. This is something you'll need.
- **Blankets or Acoustic Tiles**

Barring the computer, which hopefully you already have, you're looking at spending a few hundred dollars here. Look at this as an investment in a new hobby. People spend hundreds on cameras and video games. At least this is a hobby where you can actually make some money after you spend the money. It could even become a career! Maybe, ask for some of the items for your birthday or a holiday if you can't afford them all at once. If you really work at this, you'll make the money back; but a warning, it will be slow. I think it took me almost two years to earn back the money I initially spent on equipment and fees for auditioning sites. Don't worry, we'll get to those auditioning sites once I've finished explaining how to set-up and use your studio.

Once you have purchased and installed all of your equipment, read the guides and go through the online tutorials your equipment comes with to understand how everything works. I cannot stress enough how important it is for you to become an audio expert to work in this field.

Remember, you are running a sound studio in addition to being a voice over artist--this is your draw. This is why people want to hire you. If this seems overwhelming…it should, especially if you've never edited audio before. If you're doing it right, you should feel really out of your league and confused. I did. It simply takes time. Being uncomfortable means you are working outside of your comfort zone. Working outside of your comfort zone means you are growing and learning. In this case, being uncomfortable is good!

Your editing software is probably the most important and complicated piece of equipment in your studio. The tutorials that come with it will walk you through how to record, edit, and manipulate audio using all of the equipment you have purchased. Don't expect to get this in one day. Practice every item mentioned in every chapter of your tutorial. I like to tell people that I learned everything I know from talking to tech support. There are many tech folks out there who deserve a really nice gift basket from me.

Creating a Quiet Recording Space

In addition to your equipment, your recording area also includes the walls and space around you. Ideally, you want to have your desk in a closet or in the corner of a room--a quiet room. You can go online and search for what other voice artists have done (Google and YouTube are your best friends), but when I was first starting out, I found the most cost-effective thing to do was to use a staple gun and staple some sound-dampening blankets. I stapled the blankets to the ceiling directly above my work space and on the walls surrounding the small corner I was recording in. A great cheap way to do this is to go to a storage facility and buy a few moving blankets and use those. Moving blankets do a nice job of absorbing noise, meaning, to an extent, they stop your voice from bouncing off surfaces around you and therefore, sounding hollow. You can staple some acoustic tiles to the walls instead, sure. If you have the money, there are really cool portable vocal isolation booths like the Kaotica Eyeball (https://www.kaoticaeyeball.com/) out there these days, too.

Don't go breaking the bank, though. No, blankets won't soundproof completely, but they absolutely help. If all you can do is throw a comforter over your head right now, do it; that's good enough to start. I ended up building a recording booth later, when I had a work load that just couldn't wait any longer for the guy mowing his lawn next door to finish up. Sound blankets don't block out issues such as this.

Noise is the enemy when it comes to recording! No matter what you're using, be sure to test your space. This is easy to do. Simply put on your headphones and push "record" using your editing software. Can you hear your heat or air-conditioning running? The fan in the bathroom? If you can hear these things, your clients can hear them in the background of your audio, too--and it matters. You'll have to have these things turned off while you're recording if they make any hum or noise that can be picked up. If someone is mowing their lawn next door and you can hear it, yup, you'll have to wait for them to finish before you can record. If your chair is making clicks and pops, get a stool and stop moving so much when you read! Just work on getting the cleanest audio you can.

Mics Matter

While we're on the subject of "noise", let me briefly explain why you shouldn't use one of those handy dandy, super affordable USB mics that plug right into your computer. I'm going to explain this in total non-tech speak for you.

What I'm about to say is going to sound really counterintuitive since when you think of speaking into a mic, you think of loud noises. But the signal from a microphone into your computer is actually super-duper quiet. Why? I have no idea. It just is. It's like the calories in a good burger and one beer. We all wish it wasn't that way--it just is, and we all must deal with it.

How do you deal with it? You buy an interface to boost that signal from your mic, so your mic signal is louder when it goes into your computer. You plug your mic into the interface and the interface into the computer. This is called your signal chain.

Okay, so that's good; now you know that the signal from your mic is quiet and that you can buy an interface thing to make it stronger. Wait…you probably want to know *why* you want to make that signal stronger, right?

Here's the deal, when you record something like a commercial, you need to be able to hear it well. It can't be really quiet when you send it to the client for use. You could say, "Well, I/they have this volume knob and I/they can just turn that thingy (this is called "gain", BTW) up and my voice is louder." Yes, you/they could, and while your voice would be louder, so would that horrible fuzzy background noise that is the signature mark of "poor quality" audio. You want to boost the signal and *not* the background noise. Get it?

I'll pause for the collective groan.

Right? I hate it, too! I wish it wasn't like that, I do! But it is. Don't be embarrassed if you're just now realizing you've been presenting less-than-stellar audio to people you want to impress. I've been there. You just swallow that embarrassment right on up like that good burger and beer. It's over. Now you know better and you can move forward.

If you want to boost your microphone signal even more, you can even add a preamp to your signal chain. You don't need it starting out, but a preamp is glorious once you can afford a good one. You can whisper and the signal is still strong! You can do so much more with your voice with a preamp.

Last little note, while I'm still talking "noise" here, be sure that your computer is not directly next to your microphone. The fan in your computer is actually loud enough that it will be picked up on your mic. When I started out, I had two desks. I would work on one and have my mic there, then I had my laptop on another cheap, roll-a-way plastic desk. I would "roll" the laptop out when I started to record and "roll" it back next to me when I wanted to edit. Email your scripts to yourself and read your scripts off of your tablet or phone, as these don't create any noise in your recording area.

A FEW, QUICK, COMMON, AUDIO TROUBLE-SHOOTING TIPS FOR BEGINNERS

We're about to practice what you're going to be asked to do by voice seekers in order to get you ready for auditions! But first, I want to address a few common mistakes people make with their audio when starting out. Again, I'm using Mixcraft (http://www.acoustica.com/mixcraft/) for my examples, but these things can be applied to really any editing software. The mistakes I'm mentioning are ones I've made myself. These mistakes cost me jobs and connections, so make sure you have them mastered *before* you try to get your voice out there!

-When you record, you hear clicks or pops in the audio or your audio seems to be delayed when playing it back on your editing software.

It's most likely your latency. Search "latency" in your editing software tutorial to see how to correct this. It can take some time to find the perfect level for your system. Once you find it, leave it!

-Your audio sounds really quiet.

We know you're not using a USB mic without an interface, right? Turn up your mic gain and the output level on your audio interface. Speak louder. Also, get close to your mic while talking. You want to be about a hand's length away from your mic. Audio level is huge! Make sure your playback levels are hitting right in the middle and not going too low or up into the red. The level should be hitting a nice medium level on the bar, where you can monitor your audio level while playing back your recordings.

-You only hear your voice in one speaker or in one side of your headphones while listening back.

You need your audio to play in both channels! If you're using Mixcraft, be sure to use the drop-down arrow on your "arm" button when you "arm" to record on your audio track. You can click on "left channel" or "right channel" to get your audio to come out of both channels when recording. You'll hear the difference (hear your voice coming out of both sides of your headphones) when you play back.

TIME TO PRACTICE!

If you know how to use your equipment and are able to record and play back audio that has really nice, clear sound quality and good levels, you are ready to start training for what you'll be asked to do as a voice over artist.

What Kind of Voice Should You Use While Practicing?

Two common misconceptions people tend to have about voiceovers are that they're either all weird, cartoon voices or that they're all done by people with big, booming, announcer-type voices. There is a ton of voice work out there and which jobs you book are entirely based on what your normal voice sounds like. Don't try to sound like someone else unless it's asked of you. The beauty of your voice is that nobody else sounds like you. Just try to sound clear but conversational--like you're reading to a friend. Don't mumble, but don't over-enunciate to a point where you sound stuffy, fake, or pretentious. Just be a nice presentable version of yourself.

Voices are all around us and you're going to start noticing them. You'll hear voice over artists on the speakers at the grocery store, in radio and television commercials, in that online tutorial or product video you need to check out, on the answering machine at your doctor's office, on your yoga app, at the gas pump, in the game your child is playing, on that person's ringtone in the elevator, and so on. As you listen to these voices, you'll begin to notice how many different styles and kinds of voice projects there really are. Everyone's voice is different and you'll soon find what your voice's natural strengths are. You might sound like a mom, the guy next door, young and hip, a warm middle-aged announcer, etc. These are all voice types that are needed. You'll soon find out which category you fall into, but again, just read using your normal voice for now.

Practicing a Commercial

Radio commercials are a very common request from production houses. Let's practice what it would be like to get an order like this.

Say you auditioned for a ten-second radio advertisement (yes, we'll get to how to audition once you're ready) and now a production studio has emailed you saying that they liked your audition and want to hire you to read their spot. You have emailed back thanking them and have told them you're available. They then email you back a script with the following notes:

"Please read this in a happy tone and send us a clean, dry MP3 audio file with three takes. It needs to be exactly ten seconds. If you can get this back within the hour, that would be great."

Here is the copy.

Interested in voice overs? Want to make money from home doing something you love? Check out "How to

Become A Voice Over Artist" by Natalie Roers. Available now for your Kindle. Download today!

If you don't know how to pronounce something in the script, such as my last name in this example, see if you can find how to pronounce it by searching online. If you can't find it by searching, email and ask the client before you start. If you asked me, I would tell you my last name is pronounced like "roars" as in, "The lion roars."

What you would do now is immediately open your editing software and prepare to record. The client said they wanted you to sound happy, right? This means when you read, you need to smile. You can hear the smile in your voice. They also said they wanted the audio "clean" and "dry." "Dry" means they do not want you to hit the FX (effects) button and add any sound effects to your audio file such as compressors. The client will probably do that on their end. The client also asked for the file you send to be "clean" which means they want it edited. Clients do not need to specify this; it's usually a given. You should never turn in audio where you have not first "cleaned" it up by editing out your mouth noises and breaths.

Ready? Arm your audio track and do the read a few times until you think you have your first good take. Trim off the dead (silent) audio at the front and at the end of the sound file (this is called topping and tailing your audio) and move the audio back so that your sound starts at about half a second into your track. When you do this, look up at the timing bar on your track. Is your read exactly ten seconds? If not, you'll need to redo it until it is. Also, if you take a breath while you are reading the script, you will need to edit that breath out. Pause when you take breaths to make editing easy on yourself. If you are using Mixcraft, you will simply right click on the audio in the place where you want to cut the breath and select "split track." You would do this both at the beginning of the breath and at the end. Once you have split the track, right click on the section you isolated and select "delete" to delete your breath. Move your remaining audio together, so that it sounds like one "clean" continuous take. Nobody should ever know that you took a breath! Is your clean read ten seconds in length? Is it happy? Is it dry (no effects)? If your lips are making weird smacking noises, try drinking apple juice--this helps. Personally, my mouth is a noisy mess, so I keep a tube of "dry mouth" gel on me at all times. I also like to keep those "snoring" nose strips on hand for when I sound stuffed up. Dry mouth and nose strips--I know, this is a sexy little business, isn't it?

Saving and Sending your Practice Commercial in Different Formats

Your client also requested three takes, so try to do each take in the same style voice they liked in your audition, but use different inflections for each take. Maybe you go up in pitch on the last line in the first read, but down in pitch on the second read. Once you have three happy, clean (edited), dry (no effects), and exactly ten-second reads, you'll need to save your file in MP3 format as your client requested. In Mixcraft, you'd click on "File" and select the option to save the file as an MP3. If you have editing software that won't let you save in a format you need, go ahead and save a copy of whatever format you have into iTunes. iTunes will let you convert and save your file in virtually any format you need for free.

*One professional note about saving:** In Mixcraft, you'll notice as you're saving your file as an MP3, that you can "read the format details" here. If you want to, set them specifically (some voice over seekers ask for specific settings), you can do that by selecting "edit details" and choosing to configure your settings. I have my MP3 settings at 320 kbps mono. Additionally, my WAV settings are set at 44,100 Hz, 16 bits, mono. Feel free to set yours the same, but if you're ever asked to change them for a particular client, this is how you do it.

You will save your file as an MP3 and then email it back to your client by using the paperclip attachment in your Gmail message. Email yourself to practice this. You can use other email services, yes, but I highly suggest opening a Gmail account if you don't already have one. These accounts can send very large audio files. If for any reason you have a project too large for your Gmail account to send, you can use sites like Hightail.com to send large audio files for free.

I want you to practice recording and sending over and over again, so that you can do both within twenty minutes or less. Speed, along with quality, is essential in this game, so be sure you're a pro. Once you've practiced this enough, try writing/finding and recording a thirty-second commercial, then a sixty-second commercial. Assign yourself different tones as you record these practice commercials, such as: soft-sell (laid-back), hard-sell (high energy--think car commercials), young and hip, etc. Save the files (bump them down) as WAV files instead of the MP3 you already practiced and email them to yourself. Want great radio copy to practice with? Again,

Google is your friend, guys. Just search for new scripts to practice whenever you need.

When I first started, I would labor for hours over a ten second spot--you're normal, don't worry. This is an art. It takes time. You'll get there. And once you do get there, you'll never forget it. It's just like riding a bike. Once you can turn copy (deliver finished reads) quickly and comfortably, you're ready to make a demo for yourself. That's coming, but let me first talk to you briefly about coaches and classes.

CLASSES, COACHES, AND VOCAL TIPS, OH MY!

I'm often asked when/if voice actors should seek training and how much/with whom. There is no one-size-fits-all answer I can give on this. This business is about getting to know yourself and what you need, and we're all different. Try a bunch of different methods and see which one brings out the best in you, but *please beware of scams!*

Let's start with when/if you should seek training.

Personally, I grew up with acting and vocal coaches for film and theatre work and was coached heavily as a television personality as I got older, too. This training helped me greatly in being able to transition easily into voiceover. If you've never taken an acting or voice class, you really should as soon as you start out.

An outside perspective is a great way to catch any bad habits you may not even realize you have and, catch them before they become hard to correct.

Now, if you're like I was and have been coached your entire life, you may run into the problem of sounding over-coached. You're so used to doing everything perfectly that you lose some of the magic of just being who you are naturally--and natural is big in this business. When someone can't see you, your job is all about conveying feeling. You don't just want to sound "pretty", you also want to sound REAL. Just as you should know when you need help, you should also know when to walk away from coaching or even switch coaches to "keep it real" or get fresh, new perspectives.

How should you find a coach or class?

Start by doing a Google search for voice over classes or coaches in your area. Look at prices. Look at reviews. If you can't find an affordable or reputable class, search for online instructors. There are a ton of great instructors out there who offer training via Skype these days. There are great online courses these days, too. I've taken some terrific and very affordable ones through Gravy for the Brain, (https://www.gravyforthebrain.com/). Follow established voice actors on social media. Who do they use? Who do they talk about?

How much should you spend?

Look, you know that for yourself. Personally, I have a self-improvement fund that I set aside every year. I may use that money on demos, classes, equipment, branding, etc. I use my money in whatever way I think will serve me best that year. You might spend $500 that year or $2,000; your money is yours and you decide how best to spend it. If you really have nothing? Get creative. There are lots of free/low cost webinars out there that you can take. If you can't afford to go to a huge voice conference, see if they offer à la carte classes. Buy eBooks on Amazon for a few dollars and read up on tips from professionals. You get the deal. Social media is a great way to find out about these things. The voice over community is extremely supportive. We've all struggled to get here and we all know what it's like.

Beware of scams!

Nobody should charge you a grand for a class or make larger than life promises to you. Look around. Ask for prices from multiple people. See what's normal.

I also like to warn people to steer clear of unethical people. I won't name names, but I had a very, well-known instructor approach me (I was thrilled!) with a sales push that left a terrible taste in my mouth. This person wanted to coach me. I had just spent my money on equipment for the year and had some other big personal expenses at that time, but was very interested; I told this person such. Their response was borderline threatening. This person suggested that "without 'proper training' I was being disrespectful to the industry" and if I "wanted this bad enough, I could make it happen." They then never spoke to me again. Yuck, right? The thing is, I DID have money a few months later, but I did NOT spend it with that person.

Please do not let people pressure you into spending money you don't have. If you are choosing between feeding your kid that month and classes, feed your kid. You will not be "blacklisted" from the industry for doing so. It certainly doesn't mean you don't "want it badly enough". Choosing your child over work just means you're not a raging, narcissistic sociopath. That's a good thing, in my opinion. Any services worth their salt will be around in a few months or a year when you can afford them. Another great way to practice your reads and get unbiased feedback for free? Many voice actors are holding group practice sessions where they direct one another via Skype now. This is awesome!

In addition to classes, coaches and group directing sessions? Read! Check out Twitter, Facebook, books, articles, and blogs. Everyone has a little nugget. Keep grabbing nuggets and you'll end up with a pile of gold.

That being said, what are *some of my favorite tips and tricks that I've been able to pick up over the years?*

#1. The key to frustration? WALK AWAY!

If a read isn't working, I promise you it will not get better by your 50th pass. If after a few reads through your copy you find yourself feeling frustrated, stand up and walk into another room. Even thirty seconds can be enough time. When you sit back down, you'll sound better. Try getting up and doing a few jumping jacks if you need more energy, too. Energy in your body will translate into energy in your voice.

#2. Want to sound "warm"? Pretend you are reassuring someone.

Is someone asking you for a "warm" read? While you read the copy, picture a family member or friend and pretend you are trying to reassure them of something while reading the copy. I believe I picked this tip up from a free webinar somewhere, and it's served me very well over the years.

#3. Nailing reads aimed at children?

I had a director once, who gave me the best advice for how to nail reads that are aimed at children--pretend you're speaking to someone who doesn't know English. BAM. That one's a keeper. Trust me.

#4. Want more range in your reads?

There are lots of techniques for range, but a good rule of thumb is to go through your copy once using fluctuating voice volumes and tones; get really, really quiet, loud, low, and high in pitch. Read the copy once through in major extremes, then read the copy normally. You will naturally read with more shading as you won't be afraid to go "too far" after reading in such a crazy manner the first time. I do this all the time.

#5. Direct yourself by listening back.

Listen back to yourself performing the reads through speakers after each take. Listening back like an audience member will help you immediately identify things you don't like. Also, listen to your pitch. I read a great blog once where the author said you should go up and down by at least three notes in each script. To practice what this sounds like say,

> *I can go up, up, up*
> *I can go down, down, down*

while going up in pitch on each "up" and down in pitch on each "down".

#6. Want to sound animated? Move your body!

Still, try to keep your mouth a hand away from the mic and don't make loud noises, but try moving your hands and body when you read. Just like smiling when you read, you can hear the animation in your voice when you move your hands and face.

#7. Be a mind reader.

You don't have to be a mind reader to know what your client likes. Go to their website or look for previous commercials of their product on YouTube. You can know what kind of reads your client usually goes for by listening to what they've done in the past. This will give you a major leg up in the auditioning room.

Lastly, EXPERIMENT!

Try different things while you read. In time, you'll find your own weird tricks that are unique to you. I've found that if I pretend to put my hair in a ponytail that I give a killer natural read. I have no idea why. It works for me, though.

MAKING A DEMO

If you know how to use your equipment and have practiced and studied voice over to the point where you feel ready to start auditioning, you're going to need a demo.

A demo is just a quick, little audio compilation of your best work that you use to get jobs. You use a demo like a business card; you can hand it out to prospective clients or post it places where you can find work. Demos need to be short and fast-moving because nobody listens to your whole demo. You're lucky if a voice-seeker listens to even thirty-seconds of your demo. To get a feel for what these sound like, you can listen to my voice demos on my website natalieroers.com.

Now, since/if you haven't booked any real jobs yet,

should you get a professional demo done now or not?

This is another one of those questions you'll need to answer for yourself. Let me try to help you, though.

The trend right now is to have a different sixty-second demo for each category of work that you do: product videos, video games, commercials, IVR, promos, audiobook narration, characters, etc. There are a lot of different kinds of voice over categories out there, aren't there? Only time, practice, and auditions will tell which of these categories you'll be working in the most. I'm not going to lie, good demos can be pricey. If you're just starting out, you *should* get much better as you go, and chances are you'll hate your first demo in a year's time. It's not that I don't suggest one, but maybe just ONE demo in the category you hope to get the most work in is a safe way to start out. Just like with classes and coaches, shop around for reputable people. Some good folks I know for demos are Eric, over at Ear Blowing Audio (http://earblowingaudio.com/) and Chuck, over at Demos that Rock (http://www.demosthatrock.com/).

If you want to hold off on demos or don't have any money for one, that's okay. I don't want you to feel like you need to blow your life's savings to get into this business. Not everybody has a few grand in the bank when they start--I didn't. Professional services *do* help you, I *do* suggest them, but you should pay as you can. You can make yourself some simple demos until you're ready to replace them. I did this when I first started, and it worked fine for me.

How to Make a Demo

Let's say we're going to make a demo for commercials. Since you haven't booked any real jobs yet, you'll need to create your demo using the practice commercials you've done. Try to stay away from copy (scripts) from huge brands. Production studios are going to know you weren't the voice of the Olay campaign when you're first starting out, so don't try to act like you were; just use non-product-naming generic copy that you've written or found online to start.

If you are using Mixcraft, you would open a new recording file to start making your demo. Remember how your clients didn't want effects, but wanted dry audio? You *do* want effects on a demo. You want your demo to sound produced, so this is where you would use effects. Arm your new track using both channels, then click on "fx" on your track and select a generic compressor that you like from the drop down menu of effects. Now, you can either record your scripts again or import three of your best practice commercials by using the "add sound file" feature at the top of the page.

If you're importing your favorite reads, you'll add all of these practice commercials on the same recording track line and cut each read down to about ten or fifteen seconds. Once you've cut down your reads, you'll need to bump them all together, slightly overlapping the last half-second of each read. You create a natural fade-in and fade-out effect between the reads by doing this.

Demos also need to have music underneath the reads. In Mixcraft, you can add music by opening the loop library and searching for music beds. You would select three music beds you like--that also fit the mood of your three reads--and add them to a separate recording track line under where your commercials are. Trim these music beds and overlap them directly under your commercial reads. Make sure the audio level for the music track is set much lower than your reads. It is background music, you want to hear it, but hearing your voice is more important. Just play around with all of it until it sounds perfect! When you think you have it, go ahead and save it with a special label, such as "YourName-Commercial Demo", as both a WAV and MP3 file.

FINAL HOMEWORK

You now know how to use your equipment and have a demo! Congrats, you're almost there! At this point you'll want to do some final homework to see if you're really ready to enter the auditioning world. I say this because you only get one chance to make a first impression; make a good one! If you aren't really ready, or something is hugely wrong with your recordings that you aren't aware of, you could turn off a production studio and may never get a chance to impress them again.

For example, I booked a huge job with a great studio when I was first starting out and told them I could have their file back in thirty minutes (they were in a major rush). I took way too long recording and then couldn't figure out how to bump my recording down to a WAV file. When I did get it figured out, it was already late. Then I discovered it was too big of a file to email with my old yahoo account. I ended up using a service I wasn't familiar with and my delivery of the file was so behind what I had promised, that the production house was calling me on the phone and making me a frantic mess. Needless to say, they never called me again.

This would be the perfect time for you to find a mentor.

Please don't ask me; I'm hoping this book is enough of a guide to answer the multitude of questions I field on a regular basis. Coaches and classes are great for mentorship. You can also find and join online forums for voice artists or find a particular voice artist you like by searching demos online and approach them with an email. However you find someone, simply ask this person if they would mind listening to your demo. You'll want to ask them for their opinion on which style of voice they think you have and if your audio sounds good as far as levels and quality.

Asking someone who makes money doing this for a living is just invaluable! Remember to be polite, thank them for the time they are taking out of their day to help you, and don't ever be hostile or too clingy. You are now representing your business whenever you have contact with anyone in this industry.

A Cautionary Tale

I had a fellow ask me for advice once via email. I took a lot of time to craft a useful response right away. Not only did this fellow take two months to respond to me, but he never said thank you *and* made a point to tell me how unavailable he was when he did get back to me. This guy didn't know this, but I had just been asked for referrals for male talent from a client I worked with for a really nice gig. This guy had no idea that he was in the right place at the right time, but his wrong attitude kept me from ever passing on his name.

Study Your Competition

You should now be paying much closer attention to the voice overs that are all around you. Which are the voices you identify with? Which ones are you drawn to? Do you find one voice style especially attention-grabbing or pleasing? Google "voice over artists" and go to websites that offer voice services. These kinds of websites should have voice banks where you can listen to demos. How does your demo stack up to the demos you're listening to? Which voice over artists sound like you? Once you pinpoint which artists sound like you, pay attention to what kinds of commercials they are reading in their demos. How are their voices described on websites? These are good indicators of the types of voice jobs you would be good at and what kind of voice you would be described as having. This is important information to know, so you know what jobs to audition for!

DIPPING YOUR TOE
IN THE AUDITIONING POOL

If you have a decent demo, are confident in your recording abilities, are mentor approved, and have a pretty good idea of what "type" of voice you have, you're ready to get out there!

There are lots of ways to start getting jobs and it's ALWAYS changing. You most likely are not ready for an agent yet (I'll get to that), so to get voice over work you'll most likely want to utilize pay-to-play audition sites, freelance sites, and later, booking sites.

Pay-to-Play Audition Sites

These are sites where you can audition for voice over jobs if you pay a yearly fee to be listed on the site. Anyone can join. You pay to play. Some actors like these sites, some don't. I had a good experience with them and highly recommend them. On one of these sites, you'll be able to audition for everything from small gigs all the way up to national and international gigs. Why do I suggest them? Well, you don't exactly have the resume yet to join booking sites (we'll get to those later) and you need to get feedback from real, potential clients somehow. This also gives you access to the kinds of auditions you used to only be able to get through agents.

Auditioning sites that enable feedback allow you to grow tremendously. There are a few sites to choose from, but one of my favorites is Voice123.com. Even if you're not selected for a job, clients will "rate" your audition, so you can see how you did against your competition. Like I said before, anyone can join, but the joining fee is a little steep at a few hundred dollars for the year. Believe me, I dislike paying that much, but the number of clients I picked up through this site over the years was more than worth it. I think this fee also weeds out some of the less-serious voice talents; as a result, the clients that are booking on it tend to be of a higher caliber.

Whichever site you join, you'll need to create a profile and upload your demo. Look at other voice talents on the site and get an idea of how they are filling out their profiles. Don't be too long-winded if you don't have a ton of experience, simply state what you're good at and move on. You can fill in your profile more as you start booking jobs. This is where "knowing your voice" comes in handy. However you describe your voice is how your voice will be advertised on the auditioning sites. The descriptions you provide will also be used to match you with auditions from voice seekers in need of your particular kind of voice!

Freelance Sites

There are really great freelance sites out there that are free to join now and that even let you list your services for free. These sites are a great place to gain experience and land repeat clients. They can be frowned upon, though. Many pros feel (and rightfully so) that freelance sites drive down rates for the whole industry and put work out there that isn't exactly "quality" work. You should charge industry rates (search online to see what non-union and union rates are for voiceover work), but to get started a lot of folks offer lower rates to attract more clients and build a resume. I get that. If you are turning out quality work with quality audio and you are in demand, though, remember you are worth these standard rates. It helps you and the industry as a whole.

Booking Sites

There are free, direct booking sites out there for voice actors that are tremendous. Look at these sites like "virtual agents". You can apply to be listed on these sites. If selected, they advertise your services, clients book you directly, and the site takes a small percentage of what you make for finding you the work. I'd wait to approach these sites until after you've gotten some real work under your belt, though. Waking up with orders in your inbox and not having to chase down work is very nice.

Tips for Getting the Most Out of Your Auditions

No matter which way you go about getting jobs, you will be asked by prospective clients to audition. You should know that most pay-to-play sites only let you audition for a limited number of projects until you've proven yourself able to book jobs. In order to prove yourself as quickly as possible, I've been able to come up with a few auditioning tips and strategies that will greatly increase your odds of getting booked on or off these sites.

1. Only audition for jobs that you think you are a really good fit for. For example, I have a natural announcer type of voice from my years in broadcasting. Until I became more confident in my craft, I steered clear of auditions for testimonial-style reads as my voice naturally didn't come off as the "girl-next-door" at first. I only auditioned for announcer reads as that was my comfort zone at the time.

2. Stick to low-paying jobs at first! You probably won't get matched with six-hundred dollar budget, thirty-second spots at first, but even if you do, resist the urge to audition. I say this because you will be going up against some very seasoned talent for these auditions and this will greatly decrease your odds of booking the job. Starting out, staying in the non-paying to fifty-dollar project range, will pit you against voice over talents of the same skill level. These may be low-paying jobs, but they often lead to more voice projects. Production houses that produce low-budget spots often do a lot of them and if they like you, they may contact you directly for future spots. If you're making your own demos it would also be really great if you could add real honest-to-goodness bookings to them. Yes, you can always email your client and request a copy of their finished spot for your demo. You can also search for the finished spot online and use free apps to pull the video or audio for your demo reel. A job with a zero-dollar budget may not pay, but it can get you experience and help you create a new demo.

3. Get your audition in first! When you find an audition that you think you'd be a good match for, and it seems to be a lower-budget spot that most seasoned-pros might skip over, be sure to check how many auditions that voice seeker is looking for and how many people have already auditioned. If the voice seeker is looking for one-hundred auditions…skip it. A one-in-one-hundred chance at landing a job doesn't give you the best odds, does it? You'd have a better chance at landing a job that's only looking for twenty-five auditions. Also, if you aren't one of the first twenty people to audition, I'd skip auditioning for the spot as well. A lot of voice seekers claim they want fifty auditions, but they may only listen to the first ten or twenty applicants. You'll see what I mean when you start auditioning, but take my word on this for now.

Dealing with Rejection

Even with these tips, chances are you will not book any of your first auditions. That's normal, just consider it more practice. I said before that I like Voice123.com because it has a ranking system for voice seekers to rate the auditions they receive; there's a lot of value there. Not all voice seekers use this feature, but the ones that do might rank you when you audition. If you are using Voice123.com and have received a few stars on one of your initial auditions, congrats! That's huge! You might not have gotten the job, but they think you have a good product. This helps you to know if you're on the right track as far as picking projects that would be a good match for your natural voice talents. Try to audition for projects similar to the ones you are ranked as a good match for.

If you have submitted, say, twenty reads and still haven't gotten any rankings or feedback, don't despair, but you may want to go back to your mentor and ask them for some feedback on your auditions. The voice seekers might have thought you were fine, but not a good match for their particular projects, or you might need to re-evaluate your delivery or the kinds of jobs you are auditioning for.

You must be ready for rejection in this business. It's part of daily working life and should never be taken personally. Please do not try to directly contact a business to ask why you weren't booked. This is the fastest way to get yourself banned from a production company and possibly an auditioning site as well.

BOOKING YOUR FIRST JOB: CONGRATS, YOU'RE NOW AN ACCOUNTANT!

You'll be freaking out on the inside, but play it cool when you finally do get approached for your first paying gig. Don't gush about this being your first job; don't act like you know everything. Just be a polite, normal human-being that someone would want to work with again.

Ask for what the client needs, when they need it, and then go about doing it. When you deliver your finished audio file make sure to thank them and let them know you're happy to make any changes if needed. You can attach your invoice (this is how you get paid) in the email along with your completed audio file.

What's an invoice?

There are many invoice templates out there to choose from. Search "free invoice templates" and find one you wish to copy. I have a Word document saved on my desktop that I fill out with new information each time I have a new client. Your invoice should include your name and address at the top, who you are billing (the production company's name), what job you are billing for, and the total amount that is due to you. Expect the company that hires you to write a check or pay you via Paypal (you should have a Paypal account) within thirty to sixty days after the job is completed. If you are not paid within sixty days, feel free to contact the company and politely ask them about the status of your invoice.

Print off a copy of your invoice once you have emailed it to the production company and stick it in a folder in your office. You'll save all of your invoices in this folder to tally up at the end of the year so that you may pay taxes on the money you made. The money you make doing voice overs will be filled out as "extra income earned" on your taxes. When you're making more than five-thousand dollars a year, you'll probably want to think about registering yourself as a business.

In addition to keeping an invoice folder, I also like to keep track of my jobs and who has paid me in a document saved on my desktop. Every time I get a job, I go to this document and in red, bold font, type in the date, name of the company and project, and the dollar-amount of the project. When I send this company their invoice, I turn the font to black. When I am paid, I go to this document and take the bold off the black font. This way, at a glance, I can see who has paid me, who owes me money, and who I still haven't invoiced yet.

ADDITIONAL ITEMS TO CONSIDER AS YOU BEGIN BOOKING JOBS

As you begin booking jobs, you'll start hearing stuff about "recording remotely" or different ways you can record with clients where they can listen in live and direct you while you're recording. At first, you really won't be doing much of this. If someone wants to direct you live, you can offer to put them on Skype on your phone or just have them listen in on your cell phone while you record. But if you get to a point where you are being requested for these things a lot, you might want to consider your options.

The most popular are:

ISDN

"Recording remotely" is basically connecting your studio with someone else's. ISDN was the original way people did this. It is still used today, but now there are other less expensive options. This is a hardwire system, kind of like your home phone. Each side has to buy a special box for this to work and it costs thousands of dollars. You also have to pay monthly fees and an installation fee.

Source Connect

This system operates over the internet; it's sort of like Skype. There are expensive packages, but there's also Source Connect Now which is a free option with restrictions. This is a great option if your client will go for it.

ipDTL

This option is browser-based. For a reasonable price, ipDTL can connect with your ISDN people. It dials right into their box. It's a good option because it's affordable and easily connects for those of you who aren't tech savvy. It's as easy as connecting onto Skype or Face Time.

Local Studios

You'll definitely want to research if there are any recording studios in your area; keep that list on hand. Some clients may ask you to go to a studio instead of recording from home. If they ask you to do this, you'll need to give them the names and phone numbers of the studios closest to you so that they may book a recording window for you.

Email App

Adding the Gmail app to your cell phone is another great idea. With this app, you can set a tone to notify you when new emails come into your inbox.

You must constantly have access to email when you are auditioning for jobs. If a client contacts you and you don't respond in a timely manner, they will often choose another talent on their list to give their order to. Additionally, if you know you have a doctor's appointment or meeting and will not have access to your email for a few hours, be sure to set an "Out of Studio" automatic email response in your Gmail settings. These automatic emails let clients know why you are not responding and when you will be able to get back to them.

CREATING AN ONLINE PRESENCE

Once you begin booking auditions on a fairly regular basis, you should begin getting repeat business from people in the form of direct email bookings.

You're rolling! At this point, you might want to think about creating a professional online presence for yourself. In this day and age, many companies like to do research on the people they hire--voice seekers are no different. If you have a Facebook or Twitter page, make sure you don't have a lewd profile picture or any inappropriate material that comes up when voice seekers search your name. This should go without saying, but you'd be shocked at what I've seen.

Look at what other people are doing, come up with a catchy name and brand for yourself. Do your research. Popular, free avenues to create an online presence for yourself include creating a Facebook business page, a Twitter business account, an Instagram account, a LinkedIn page, and a Google+ account--which even comes with a YouTube channel you can use to showcase some of the projects you've done.

It's also great to have a website where voice-seekers can learn more about you and check out more samples of your work. Feel free to check mine out at natalieroers.com. I do work in a few other areas as well, so I use my name as my brand; this way I can post everything that I do in one place.

Branding is another one of those professional services that I *do* recommend you pay for, but I understand most of you won't have the money when you first start. If you don't have money to hire someone yet, I suggest picking a domain name for your website, registering it somewhere like GoDaddy.com, and building your own website at a place like Wix.com. You can create and maintain a website for less than a hundred dollars a year by going this route. If you don't like the stigma of using a cheap or free site-building service (I feel ya), you can usually pay a little bit extra to take the site's branding off your page so nobody knows who built it for you. I'd pay for that option if possible. It's a small thing you can do to make your business look "higher-end".

Maintaining Proper Online Etiquette

Business sites and social media accounts should share your personal thoughts and photographs--to an extent. You want people to get to know you as a person, but remember you are running a business. If you want to be seen as a professional that people take seriously and respect, you need to present yourself in that manner. Do not share explicit material, hate-filled rants, shots of you in your bathing suit, or a million obnoxious selfies on your business accounts. You also shouldn't talk about yourself as if you are God's gift to the voice over world or put down other voice over talents. Putting down others does not make your own star shine any brighter. These same rules apply to your email correspondences with clients.

The client is always right. They are running the show, not the other way around. Remind yourself of the fact that there are a ton of voice talents out there to choose from and you can easily be replaced. You should always remember how lucky you are that your clients are choosing YOU and that you are making great money doing something you love. Be someone that you, yourself, would want to work with. Don't let people abuse you, but you know what I mean.

While you're at it, please make sure to have someone knowledgeable proof-read your online accounts. Not only will you be working with writers on a regular basis, but your business is essentially built on being able to clearly convey messages. That being said, I don't think it's necessary for me to further explain why it's so important not to have egregious spelling and grammatical errors on your sites.

GROWING A CLIENT BASE

When I started making over five-thousand dollars a year (this took about three years), I began to get serious about turning my hobby into a full-time business. There are many ways to grow when you are ready to branch out from solely using auditioning sites.

Join Direct Booking Sites

I mentioned those direct booking sites earlier; you're ready for them now! There are lots of websites that allow voice-seekers to book voice over talent directly through their sites. Just search "find voice over talents" and see how many pop up. If you're an experienced voice talent, there should be a place on these websites to submit your demo for consideration to be listed with them. These sites don't charge you anything to be listed with them, but since you are being booked through these sites and you don't have to audition for the jobs you get, the host site takes a percentage of the money you make through them.

When you're ready, join as many of these direct booking sites as you can. You'll begin to make new connections through these sites--just as you have done and continue to do--through auditioning sites.

Increase Your Hours

For many of you, you will be working a different full-time job as your voice over career is taking off. While your "day job" gives you financial security, unfortunately it also prevents you from growing your business. Not that I recommend leaving your day job, but I'm going to be honest: you might hit a wall in growth when you are unavailable to record during normal business hours.

Production studios are open during normal business hours and many cannot wait until evening for their audio.

While they might like your voice, they might skip over selecting you for jobs if you aren't available when they need you. This is something you really need to consider when your objective is to get to the next level. I was terrified when I left my job in broadcasting to pursue voice overs full-time, but once I was available to work during the day, my work load more than tripled in just the first month.

Cold Email Production Studios

Once I was available full-time for voice overs and had a few years of experience under my belt, I started to grow my business even more by cold-emailing production companies. There is a great site called ProductionHUB.com that has listings for thousands of production companies. I went to this site and one by one looked up companies, searched their sites to see if they offered voice overs or produced commercials, and searched for a name of someone in production and their email address. This is time-consuming, yes, but I did this every day for about a month and came up with a huge list of potential clients.

Once I had my list, I created personal emails to each of these contacts and individually sent them very short messages that stated how I was a full-time voice over artist, offered great rates, and that I'd love to work with them if they were ever in need of my voice type. Attached in the email were my rates and my demo.

I can't tell you how many new clients I was able to pick up this way. Maybe one out of every six production companies responded. It might have taken them months to contact me, but they kept my email and information.

You can cold email anyone with your information. Don't be afraid to approach people! Chances are your friends and family all work at businesses that advertise. I've heard of people having success by doing things like looking up the YouTube channels of local businesses and finding/ approaching the ones whose videos only had music and could use voice over.

There's no wrong way to find work! Get just as creative with your sales as you are with your voice over work.

STARTING A BUSINESS

Let's say you are taking the leap and are making enough money to go full-time into voice over. You are probably making enough to have grown out of the "extra income" bracket on your taxes.

Becoming a Sole Proprietor is the easiest self-employed business tax category to navigate. Do some research on it, but you'll most likely need to go to a registration center for small businesses in your city or county. You'll register your business and pay for a license at this center. It's a bit time-consuming, but relatively inexpensive. Once you have your license, you'll want to open a small business account through your bank to deposit your earnings into; businesses cannot mingle business income with personal accounts, so this is essential.

Once you have your license and have opened a business account, you'll need to register with the IRS online to pay quarterly taxes on the money you are making. Uncle Sam can hit you hard at the end of the year, so you want to make sure you're paying taxes! All the information is online and you can pay at the click of a button, so just read about it and get up to speed.

Becoming a business has many tax advantages and it allows you write off office and equipment expenses! In some cases you can even write off expenses for the portion of your home you use for a studio. I have a blog (http://www.natalieroers.com/blog) entry dedicated to taxes on my website that should help you out should you ever need it.

SPREADING YOUR WINGS

As you make more money, invest in yourself and your business. Spread those wings and fly!

Upgrade!

Now is when you start paying for those professional services to replace the free work you've done for yourself. Get some business cards made, upgrade your equipment, grow your social media presence, upgrade your website, get professional demos made, advertise, you might even need to invest in a sound proof booth (I built my own!) if you don't already have one.

Whatever you do, don't ever get too comfortable. Don't be idle with your time. If you don't have any bookings in the morning, spend that morning auditioning or cold-emailing.

Network!

Once you've made it to the point where you're making a living doing voice overs, you'll have spent so much time in your booth, you'll no doubt be feeling a little isolated–no pun intended—okay, maybe I intended it a little.

It's so cool to find other people like you out there– and there are lots of them! There are networking groups and conferences popping up all over. VO Atlanta (https://voatlanta.me/) is a really cool conference for members of the voice acting community in the United States, so is the That's Voiceover! Career Expo (http://sovas.org/about/) put on by SOVAS (http://sovas.org/home-vaa/) (The Society of Voice Arts and Sciences) – that also puts on the Voice Arts Awards (http://sovas.org/about-vaa/) every year. For voice over artists, the Voice Arts Awards are like the Oscars for voice actors.

Speaking of awards…

Awards

I can tell you from personal experience that it is a dream come true in every single way to be all dressed up and accept an award on stage for your work from a couple of celebrities. I mean, doing this for a living is the real prize, yes, but when your peers say "good job" to you in this kind of way... it's so freakin' cool. It's also a great way to network and market yourself. Awards can serve as a nice, little professional stamp of approval for prospective clients.

Anyone can enter an award show! You usually have to pay an entry fee, though, so you want to be sure that you think your work is award-worthy. Save your best pieces from the year and then look up contests where voice over actors can submit their work. Your local ADDY and PromaxBDA competitions are a great place to start. The Voice Arts Awards (http://sovas.org/about-vaa/) are wonderful, too, as they have categories for just about every type of voice work.

Like I said, awards shows are a great place to network with people that could use your services, so bring your business cards! You'll really enjoy spending time and getting to know your community at these events.

The Voice Over Actor Community

I have never worked in a warmer/more supportive community. This is a fun line of work and the people in it reflect that. Get to know the people behind the events. Here in the United States, you'll probably not meet two more glamorous, helpful, talented, kind, and inspiring movers and shakers than Joan Baker and Rudy Gaskins (http://thatsvoiceover.com/author/rudy/).

Agents

Did you let out your breath when you read the subheading above? I know, you *want* an agent–they want *you*, right?

I'm gonna get really real here, guys. Agents *do not want you* until you are a professional. But you have raw talent? Okay, approach them. If you hear nothing back, then listen to my advice. Agents are your VERY last step. You should have an illustrious resume, flawless branding, really pro demos, a nice following, some awards under your belt, and then throw some pixie dust and magic on top of that to make you stand out above the others that have all those same things, too. When you have these things, you may approach agents at events, by email, by social media, etc.

Are you sad over what I just said? Well, maybe you won't be when I drop another truth bomb on you: getting an agent does not make you rich.

You can get a few agents if you wish (in different regions of the country) and that's great. They will advocate for you and get you access to some really nice auditions–they could even land you a great series! But, for the most part, you'll still be making most of your money through your own contacts when you get an agent.

There's something really cool about this reality when you've worked to make your own business, though. There are glamorous, raw talent, SAG-card carrying, folks out there who have had their big-time agent land them a starring role in an animated feature, but still have to wait tables to make ends meet. There's NOTHING wrong with that. But if you've gotten into this industry after building your own home business, you're usually working a really nice nine-to-five from home doing nothing but creative work to pay your bills. You might have something that movie star is envious of. Regular creative work is the goal, right?

SAG-AFTRA

Let me address the "SAG" buzz word above. You might be asked to join the SAG-AFTRA union after working on more than one union project.

Should you? This is another choice that will be totally up to you.

If you go union, you'll hear that you can no longer work non-union jobs (which many of your clients might happen to be), but there are options like Fi-Core, you might want to look into. Ask yourself questions like: Do you think you'll get more union work than non-union? Do you live in a town or area that offers more union work? Do you need health care?

Joining a union is a personal decision that you make for yourself and there is no right or wrong answer.

All this talk about agents, SAG, and movie stars conjures up images of Hollywood, doesn't it? Should you move as you're spreading those wings of yours? Another deeply personal question, but you don't have to, no.

But aren't all the jobs in NY and LA?

Once upon a time this was true, but technology swooped in like an eagle on steroids and changed the entire voice over landscape over the last decade.

I actually now look at some of the people that say NY and LA have all the work, as being slightly provincial. Sure, you can live in a big city, but if you never leave it, you miss out on an even bigger world out there. There's a lot of money exchanging hands in many different ways when it comes to voice over these days and the person that snubs their nose at that, is missing out.

How long is it going to take to make it?

People are always telling me how they are going into voice over, but they *need* to make it full-time within a year, so they can quit their current job.

It's good to plan, but it's very hard to give yourself a definitive timeline when it comes to making a living in the Creative Arts. The best way to enjoy this (and make it) is to look at voice over like a hobby–a fun, hobby that happens to pay, a hobby that might one day become how you make a living. Take the pressure off yourself and you will stick with it longer. Here's the thing, it's not always the most talented person that makes it--a lot of times it's simply the person that sticks around after everyone else has given up that makes it.

I've made so many wonderful connections in this field that I've been able to branch out into other careers I'd never have even imagined for myself. This is the entertainment business after all and there are a lot of strange and wonderful opportunities. Please know, there are a ton of people and services out there that I love (or have yet to meet!), that are not mentioned here. Just see who I'm connected to on social media. Jump into the network! New auditioning sites, opportunities, and networking groups are always popping up. Constantly search and stay up-to-date on what's hot and "buzzing".

After over 10,000 hours of paid work in this field, I'm supposedly qualified as enough of an expert to give advice, but that doesn't mean that I'm done learning or that I'm the only one you should listen to.

I'm certainly not the only person in this field who has written a reference book, so pick up all the books you can! I've simply shared the way I "made it" in this guide, and that could be completely different from the way someone else made it. Their advice might even work better for you! As they say, there's more than one way to skin a cat--which I've never actually tried because it sounds utterly horrifying–but you know what I mean. There's absolutely more than one way to succeed in voice over. Reading everything you can will make you a more well-rounded talent, and that's never a bad thing.

I hope this guide has helped you along your journey! It has been my pleasure to share my experiences, and I wish you nothing but the best as you move forward into this fun and creative field.

Natalie

If you enjoyed this book, please post a review at your favorite online bookstore.

ABOUT THE AUTHOR

Natalie Roers is both a Voice Arts® Awards and PromaxBDA-winning voice over artist, award-winning author (*Lucid, How to Become a Voice Over Artist, Beneath Them*), screenwriter (*Beneath Them*), and veteran Emmy-winning television and radio personality (KCJJ, KAAL, WLTX). Natalie lives with her family in Columbia, South Carolina.

Check out all of Natalie's latest work at
natalieroers.com

Printed in Great Britain
by Amazon